What the butler saw

~ and all that

A PICTORIAL HISTORY OF
SOUTHPORT'S HISTORIC PIER

ISBN
0-9554780-0-6
978-0-9554780-0-0

Published by Harold Brough, 118 Roe Lane, Southport, Merseyside PR9 7PJ
Printed by The Copy Shop, 48 Bucks Road, Douglas, Isle of Man IM1 3AD Tel:01624 622697

LORD FEARN OF SOUTHPORT

Councillor for Norwood Ward

Tel: 01704 228577
Fax: 01704 508635

Norcliffe,
56 Norwood Avenue,
Southport,
PR9 7EQ

The new Pier, of which I am justly proud, has proved to be a great hit with the millions of visitors and residents who tread the boards each year. But how many stop to think of the interesting past which belongs to this historic Southport structure?

"What the Butler Saw and All That" provides the answer and combines history, stories, details and anecdotes to warm the cockles of your heart.

From the very early years through the Victorian, Edwardian, Georgian and Elizabethan eras, the pier has stood the test of time and managed to stave off even politicians who tried to demolish it in the early Sefton days. Thankfully it was saved and almost rebuilt with the help from Lottery Funding and will now, under its present maintenance structure agreement, last for another 100 years or longer.

This book is pure magic, a good read and will linger in your mind for time immemorial.

Ronnie Fearn

Contents

Seaside Piers 5

The First Piers 11

The Pier Boom 17

The Day Dawned 23

Spectacular Success 29

Fun Times 41

Rough Times 47

The Work Begins 51

The Pier Reopens 59

Memories of Southport Pier 63

The Mexico Lifeboat Disaster 73

The Natural History of the Pier 77

The Future of the Pier 79

Acknowledgements 80

What the butler saw

~ and all that

A PICTORIAL HISTORY
OF SOUTHPORT'S HISTORIC PIER

P IERS, or rather seaside piers, are a great British oddity. Who else would build wide, long, high-level platforms on stilts across the sands and water to nowhere in particular?

The answer is no one quite like the British.

In the huge extravagances and enthusiasm of the Victorian era they sprouted around the coasts of Britain like, well, as one who wrote of Southport's pier put it, "like a giant centipede creeping across the sands."

Not all survived. At the turn of the 19th century there were almost 100 of these grand structures. Some went up in flames. Some were battered by passing shipping. Many, pulverised by years of gales and waves, blasted by the corrosive cocktail of salt water and sand, simply surrendered in the unequal struggle and collapsed into the seas.

Southport Pier mid 19th century with a waiting pier taxi.
(Pic. Botanic Gardens Museum, Sefton Council).

Viewed from the sea, a pier and beach scene in the 19th century. Note the bathing huts used to protect the modesty of those taking the waters. "Bathing machines," as they were first called, were introduced at the British seaside about 1730. (Pic. Sefton Council).

Now just more than 50 remain, which does not necessarily mean they are open to the public.

Southport's historic pier is not merely part of the great boom in pier building in the 19th century but has a special place in the seaside history of Britain and our rich island heritage.

Even by the standards of the Victorian age it is a superb piece of design and engineering, the longest in the country when it was built, the first iron pier in the British Isles.

Some piers were built for commercial reasons, to serve shipping. But this was the first pleasure pier, built for promenading, to take the sea breezes and, in the years ahead, for pier strollers to enjoy the concerts and entertainments.

Southport's pier was useful to the fishing fleet too. But essentially this was a pier made for fun and whether its attraction was the end-of-the pier shows or the means of a bracing walk above the tide, across many decades it has brought immense pleasure to townsfolk and holidaymakers.

Like others, it came close to collapsing into the sea or being reduced to scrap iron.

But it survived, seas and storms of great fury, years of neglect and other misfortunes. It has been lengthened and shortened, closed and opened. It has survived three major fires among others. Finally, rotting and rusting, it was the subject of a heated political debate about whether, in the modern age, a seaside pier was worth the expense of a big repair bill.

The steamers and the fishing fleets had long sailed into history. The era of the amusement arcades and the What-the-butler-saw slot machines had long passed. No longer did citizens in their Sunday best walk the pier, laze in deck chairs on summer afternoons, listening to the singer offering 'We'll Gather Lilacs,' her words snatched away on the breeze. The days when George Formby, father and son, Vera Lynn, Gracie Fields and others played here were also part of a bygone age never to be recalled.

Steamers at the pier head and the opening of the pier ceremony in 1860. (Pics. Sefton Libraries and Botanic Gardens Museum, Sefton Council)

For some the old pier was an anachronism in the modern age, a platform where, curiously, the British at the seaside walked above the sands and sea to the pier end and back again perhaps to travel on a steamer or to listen to a concert and, if not, then for no obvious reason other than the exercise and to enjoy the fresh air.

Some thought the pier was simply a folly, a piece of Victorian flippancy, a wild extravagance from a different age, not worth restoring in cost-conscious times.

If such views had won the debate the demolition gangs would have been sent to work on the pier. Either that or it would have collapsed onto the sands, into the boating lake and sea.

HERE I AM
VERY MUCH IN THE PINK!

All that would have been left would be the faded newspaper cuttings telling of an exciting, lost time, of the pleasure steamers calling at the end of the pier, the fishing fleets, the famous names of the stage at the pier theatre, the side shows and the daring pier divers, among them "Professor" Powsey, set on fire before he rode his bamboo bicycle into the sea.

There would have been left just memories, of Punch and Judy shows, penny slot machines, candy floss stalls, kiss-me-quick hats, barrel-organ music, ice-creams and the train rattling towards the far end where fortune tellers opened a glimpse into the future, promising shy teenage girls that one day they would indeed meet a tall, dark stranger and live happy ever after.

But other voices, more optimistic about the future for the old pier, won the debate. The pier was not only saved but has now been restored, given a new future for the 21st century.

This is the story of one of Britain's greatest piers, the oldest and longest surviving pleasure pier in Britain, the first cast-iron leisure pier, how it was conceived and built, its changing fortune and how a precious part of our island heritage was saved and indeed virtually rebuilt.

It is a most worthwhile achievement. The pier is a valuable inheritance from the past, an elegant legacy from a lost age of splendour, and its loss would have been considerable. It seems unlikely we will ever again build a real seaside pier.

The happy result, now again bringing thousands every season to enjoy the stroll above the sands and seas, much as they did more than a century ago, has been brought about with money and some remarkable bits of good fortune.

The pier was built out of a great act of faith in the middle of the 19th century and has been saved by another. Its story has come full circle. At the close of the 20th century, it was saved, lovingly restored, by others with a similar sense of pride, determination and a new exciting vision for the future of the pier.

Professor Powsey's sensational Dive on a Bamber... Cycle.... Southport Pier Daily.

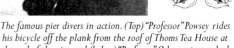

The famous pier divers in action. (Top) "Professor" Powsey rides his bicycle off the plank from the roof of Thoms Tea House at the end of the pier and (below) "Professor" Osborne is watched by elegantly dressed spectators including a little girl. (Pics. Sefton Council).

An unusual view of the Pier Head taken from the sea in the 1860s. Steps leading down to the water allowed steamers and fishing boats to use the pier at different states of the tide. (Pic. Botanic Gardens Museum, Sefton Council).

THE FIRST PIERS

THE first piers were not built for fun days by the seaside but for practical reasons, to span the gap from beach or riverbank, to reach deep water and a waiting boat, simple structures, we imagine, not much more than a plank.

Indeed perhaps there were two planks for Noah to get his animals, two by two, into his ark. So, stretching the imagination, Noah's walkway could have been the world's first pier.

Such fanciful thoughts apart, the National Piers Society 'Guide to British Piers' suggests the origins of piers can be dated to 13BC in Caesara. More convincing evidence shows that piers, like harbours, were part of Egyptian, Roman and Greek history.

But no one built piers with the enthusiasm of the British and not just slippery planks either.

As in ancient history, the first piers were just landing stages to get passengers on and off boats. The first passengers on the steamships had faced risky times. In places where there was not even a wobbly gangplank they were carried on and off the ships on the backs of hefty porters. An open boat, launched from the shore, was a luxury. But inevitably there were occasions when the beach was littered with luggage, when passengers were dumped in the sea as the porter's legs buckled under the weight or the surge of the tide. Landing piers were a priority.

Later came the pleasure piers, no longer just slippery walkways, but impressive features of design and engineering, places with entertainment, amusement arcades, kiss-me-quick hats, theatres, stage stars, end-of-the-pier artists, deckchairs and whelks, ice-cream, fish and chips and always the sea breeze and shriek of the seagulls.

Here, at weekends and in summer particularly, piers were part of the great escape at the seaside and especially for those whose weekday world was spent in the drudgery of industrial Britain in the 19th century.

Long before the age of bikinis or indeed the one-piece swim suits, fully-dressed young ladies take to the waters off the pier.

Just for a short time, men from the factories and mines, girls from the mills, could have happy hours, walk the pier with the waves beneath their feet, smell the sea, enjoy the visions to distant horizons. It was the next best thing to a real sea voyage and all for a few pence. By the 1860s and 1870s, two piers a year were being built.

Others had different reasons for joining the great trek to the coast. "Taking the waters" at inland spas such as Bath had long been popular. But the virtues of sea water too had been advanced as early as 1750 and bathing in and indeed drinking sea water was believed to cure all kinds of ills, a faith so strong that 18th century England developed a craze for sea bathing.

In 'Seaside Piers' Simon Adamson suggests that hypochondria was a popular pastime in the upper echelons of British society in the 1800s and the pier boom helped cater for those with real or imagined ills. By the end of the 18th century going to the coast was a new fashion among the rich and Southport had become one of the most fashionable watering places in the country. Its popularity was helped by the climate, described in a town guide of 1874 as "most conducive to the progress of convalescent patients."

The rapid development also of pleasure piers was such that, writing at the close of the 19th century, Henry Dawson, author of 'English Piers,' observed: "We have a craving for amusement and the end of it is that a seaside resort can only be popular when an enormous amount of capital has been expended on what is called developing it."

He referred to the immense amount invested in pleasure piers, the gigantic sums John Bull (the character symbol of British determination) was prepared to spend every summer on his pleasures. As the resorts boomed the railways made it possible for the working classes to get to the seaside.

So piers served different functions. For some they were part of the passion for "taking the waters," for others a happy day out surrounded by sea, sand and the sounds of laughter and for others, including those on the urgent business of earning a living, they were essentially a station for the steamers.

Often the best way to get to the resorts was by sea. Indeed for travellers between Southport and Blackpool and the North Wales coast the sea crossing was easier than either road or rail.

Long before a real pier was imagined, as early as the 1820s, sailing boats were operating from Southport to Blackpool and Liverpool and by 1835 the Enterprise, the first steamer, had arrived at the pier.

A keen-eyed visitor that year recorded: "Boats at high water every morning depart for Lytham, besides others which ply regularly for private hire.

"To get some half a dozen ladies on board was part of the day's adventure for, as the tide was not yet sufficiently high, it was indispensable that they should be carried in men's arms for some distance towards the boats. The young gentlemen of the party very gallantly proffered their assistance."

Southport recognised the need for a pier to reach low water, not particularly to spare the indignity and probably occasional blushes of manhandled Victorian matrons and refined young ladies but because of the huge boom in coastal traffic.

The problems of sea passengers had been recognised even in the first half of the century when local fishermen had built a long jetty to help them on and off the pleasure steamers when the tide was not sufficiently high for boats to reach the sands by the Promenade.

The jetty also provided a walkway across the beach or water. Those who wanted a close-up sea experience but not the voyage could pay, in some cases one penny or in others a halfpenny, and literally walk the rickety planks.

They were indeed slippery. Edwin Beattie, the artist who came to Southport in 1852, aged 11, remembers a frail, wooden structure, usually in need of repair after the winter storms before the new summer season. Battered by the winds and tides, sections were regularly demolished, swept away as mere driftwood. The old jetty finally collapsed into the sands.

But whether by walking the planks or accepting the offers of strong young men, thousands of passengers came to use the services such as that to Lytham, fare one shilling return.

The sea trade developed so fast that Southport had three steamship companies including the Steam Packet and Floating Bath Company, which also produced the imaginative, yet doomed scheme for a floating swimming bath off the new pier. Its supporters included the gentlemen who wrote of the value and importance of bathing in the open sea in such bright, clear and beautifully green waters as is found at the far end of the new pier head in preference to bathing in mud and sand.

The steamer trade was to extend to about 20 companies and individual operators providing almost 50 services from Southport to 15 ports and resorts.

By the 1850s, one decade before the huge explosion in pier building, local men of enterprise and vision were promoting two different schemes for a substantial pier at Southport.

One was for a pier which would provide for the passengers and goods arriving by the steamers, a commercial pier linked to the railways, a means of moving goods to Manchester and the surrounding area, a step towards the development of Southport as a genuine port, by-passing Liverpool.

Steamers at the pier head. The age of steamers at Southport pier ended in the early 1920s. (Pic. Sefton Libraries).

The second idea was simply a fun pier, a right-angled extension off the Promenade, a breezy walk seaward for townsfolk and the increasing number of visitors arriving by the trains.

Fortunately for the future development of the town as a holiday resort it was the pleasure pier vision which gathered support. The idea of a commercial pier linked to the railways was never more than a dream.

By 1860s pier rivalry was at such fever pitch in the coastal towns of Victorian England that the size and splendour of the structure was not simply a barometer of engineering achievement but of the actual success and prosperity of the town itself.

Nowhere was confidence higher, civic pride greater, than in Southport in the mid 19th century. The town would have not just the longest pier in the country, the first true pleasure pier, but a pier built by one of the greatest engineers of the Victorian age.

As it would be described at the opening, on a day of great ceremony when the wine flowed at the evening banquet and the townsfolk reflected happily on the latest addition to their lovely town, it would be "a pier unequalled in the entire kingdom."

Beach boys in their Sunday best and steamers at the Pier Head.

THE PIER BOOM

The pier boom was fuelled by the developing seaside resorts and the railways which would bring people from the industrial towns of Britain. But it was also greatly helped by the improved construction methods for iron structures and pile-driving techniques, which had been developed in response to the need to build the railways.

In Southport, even after the old jetty had collapsed into the sea, the idea of a new and substantial pier was encouraged by the town's Improvement Commissioners and backed by enthusiastic supporters and in particular Alderman Samuel Boothroyd.

But progress was slow. In 1852 a Pier Committee was established but six years were to pass before a public meeting at the town hall where Boothroyd founded the Southport Pier Company.

An early view of the entrance at the new pier. (Pic. Sefton Libraries).

Suddenly there was a greater sense of urgency about the pier project. The capital of the company was fixed at £8,000, the approved cost of the pier, later increased to £10,000 and a prospectus and shares issued.

The following year, on August 14th 1859, watched by a large crowd, the first pile of the country's first cast-iron pier was driven. The designer was the brilliant railway engineer James - later Sir James - Brunlees, of London, the contractors W&J Galloway of Manchester.

Brunlees was a Scot, born at Kelso in 1816, who had left school at the age of 12 to become one of the greatest civil engineers of his time. His great structures included docks and railways, lines around West Lancashire and Liverpool among others, and piers, including that at Southend.

He worked with Charles Douglas Fox, an engineer for the Mersey Railway, which opened in 1886 and included the 3,820-yard tunnel, an achievement that earned both men a knighthood. In a distinguished career Brunlees also became engineer to the original Channel Tunnel Company when that bold idea first appeared in the second half of the 19th century.

Horse riding on the beach with bathing huts for those enjoying the waters. In this scene in 1874. (Sefton Libraries).

He was accustomed to a tough working environment. Eight years before coming to Southport he had been in Brazil, making a railway through dense, featureless jungle. Back in England he had worked on the hostile, exposed sands across the Kent estuary, building the viaduct there and across the Leven estuary, in Cumbria.

The ingenious building techniques he pioneered there, known as jetting, he used also to build Southport's pier, working, as on the viaducts on the Ulverston railway, with the Galloway contractors.

The superstructure for the country's first iron pier at Southport was to be supported on cast-iron columns, each of

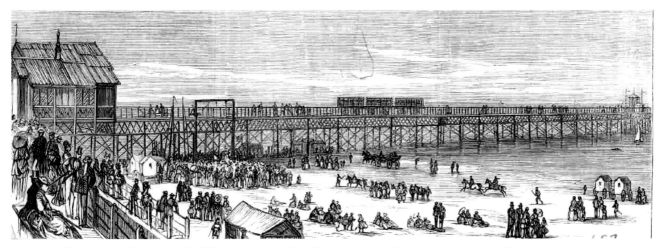

A beach gathering by the pier in the 19th century, elegantly-dressed ladies, gentlemen in bowlers and top-hats and working class men and women

three sections. To drive them down to the required depth and secure them tight in the sand, the bottom section of each column was made with a disc, 18 inches in diameter, with flanges, like scrapers at the bottom. Each disc had a hole in the centre.

A rubber tube, connected to the town's water main, snaked across the sands to the first of the cast-iron columns. There it was connected to a length of two-inch iron gas tubing, passing down the top the middle of the column, protruding about four inches through the hole in the disc at the bottom and into the sand.

The iron column was held upright by a travelling crane. The water, switched on at the mains, surged down through the iron pipe at 50 pounds per square inch pressure. As workmen, equipped with something like giant pliers, rotated the upright columns back and forth, the water gushed out of the bottom, forcing the sand away.

Slowly, without the restriction of the sand, helped by the men's to-and-fro twisting motion on the column and the scraper at its base, the column sank under its own weight.

When it had reached the required depth the water was switched off and the iron pipe carrying the water quickly withdrawn.

The sand returned around the base of the column to hold it in such a vice-like grip that within five minutes the column could hold a weight of twelve tons on the upper end with no further sinking. The first pile was put down on August 14th 1859.

The start had been delayed by bad weather and there was a further hold-up caused by a re-think about whether the construction had sufficient strength. After an examination the girder work was strengthened.

But Brunlees's clever idea for securing the columns was not only effective. It produced fast and economical results. Piles could be sunk 15-20 feet within half an hour or less, a dozen within a day and in just one week the pier advanced 450 feet towards the sea.

The horses strained and sweated, even in the winter gales, hauling the great iron columns and girders, the piles of timber decking across the sands, further out to sea as the pier advanced. Even when the beach remained covered by the sea Galloway's men continued to work from rafts, fixing the piles. Within six weeks all 237 piles were fixed in place.

After the delayed start, the bitter winds and rains of that winter caused further delays. But within less than a year the pier was finished.

It measured 1,200 yards and five yards wide, with a platform 120 feet by 20 at the sea end and with steps leading

Promenade walkers at the pier entrance. (Pic. Sefton Libraries).

down to the sands. Eight years later it would be extended to 1,460 yards. The estimate had been £10,000 but the actual cost was £9,319 - £7 13s 4d in pre-decimal money - per lineal yard and that included a toll house, two turnstiles registering the visitors, a pair of gates nine feet wide and work on the approaches from the Promenade.

The total construction was both elegant and tough, built to withstand the greatest excesses of weather, the fury of the sea. Each column had been protected against rusting by being boiled for an hour in a mixture of tar and asphalt. The cast-iron handrails were painted in red lead and then given extra protective coatings. The deal planking was dipped in boiling coal tar and then sanded.

An issue of the Manchester Examiner of 1860 described the pier as "large and substantial, but light and elegant." Also, most importantly, in the great rivalry around the coast of Britain to build bigger and better piers and so enhance a resort's reputation, it was also Britain's longest pier until Southend's extended pier opened.

The opening ceremony was fixed for August 2nd 1860. It would be a day when civic pride boomed, of ceremony and celebration, probably the greatest day in Southport's history.

THE DAY DAWNED

T HE day dawned with dismal weather, an improvement on that of the previous day but still with strong winds and skies of slate grey. But nothing would hinder the joyful celebrations of the coming hours.

From early morning and throughout almost every part of town there were signs of great activity.

Traders and employees had been busy putting up ladders against walls, the fronts of houses and shops, hanging out decorations of all kinds, making beautiful arches from the bright flowers of high summer and mixed with evergreens. A great arch was erected at both ends of the Promenade, three more on Lord Street, together with a full-length portrait of Queen Victoria and Price Albert.

The decorations around town included bright flags and

The pier opening ceremony in 1860. (Pic. Sefton Libraries)

banners and, among them, those at the pier entrance with messages proclaiming "Welcome Strangers" and "Success to the Pier Company."

The first excursions brought visitors, distinguished guests, ladies in crinolines, men in top hats, along with the workers from the factories and shops, mills and offices, from Manchester, Preston, Liverpool and elsewhere, thousands on a special day out to the seaside for joyous celebrations for what the official programme described as the "new Iron Pier." They joined the huge crowd already in the town centre.

Normal business came to a virtual halt. Nearly every tradesman stopped work for the day and the shops closed in response to an appeal from the directors of the Pier Company to make it possible for their employees to take part in the procession, indeed in what was called "the greatest and most exciting event" ever celebrated in Southport's history.

The grand, colourful procession lined up at the town hall, police officers, the band of the 3rd Royal Lancashire Militia in full uniform, directors and shareholders of the company, clergy and magistrates, residents and visitors and the fife and drums band of the 13th Lancashire Rifles. The procession set off north along Lord Street, up Seabank Road and south towards the pier entrance where, oddly for those watching, it did not turn right onto the pier or even come to a halt. But then this was an occasion not to be hurried but rather for the grand moments of pageantry and pride to be expanded and savoured.

So with flags waving, the military bands playing, the marchers continued beyond the pier entrance, down Coronation Walk, turning now north along Lord Street to approach the pier from Nevill Street where the police struggled to clear a path through the dense, wildly-cheering crowds.

Finally the procession reached the pier where three verses of the National Anthem was sung before reaching the platform at the far end where Dr. G.B. Barron, chairman of the new Pier Company, made a speech of elegance, humour and boundless civic pride.

The pier had provoked much thought and produced anxiety but he and his colleagues of the Pier Company had not been motivated by "sordid pecuniary interests" but more noble ideals. With the confidence from the great engineering achievement around him, aware of the status and influence it would bring to the town, he enjoyed a self-mocking tone about the resort.

He recalled the time, six decades earlier, when Southport was a nameless locality, the habitat of rabbits and seagulls, what might be called a miserable wilderness. Now there was a beautiful town with a pier, the new status symbol among Britain's resorts, "unequalled in the entire kingdom."

Even the climate was unmatched for mildness and indeed the once howling wilderness could challenge any part of Queen Victoria's dominion for beauty and atmosphere. The pier, the longest in the kingdom, reflected the prosperity of the town he called the "Montpellier of England."

The phrase had been used by the distinguished physician Dr. Joseph Brandreth of Liverpool. Perhaps in the celebratory mood no one noticed or indeed cared that the old French cathedral and university town was not even on the coast. But then the comparison was perhaps justified on the basis that it was a centre for the study of medicine and Southport too had the beneficial properties of its waters, "the largest and most popular watering place on the western coast of England" as it was described in a guide of 1869.

The steamer Storm King waited just off the pier to take passengers on an excursion, priced two shillings and sixpence or, for those who were also having luncheon, 15 shilling, including wine. But the wind and tides prevented the steamer coming sufficiently close for passengers to board. The more enthusiastic who tried to reach the steamer by open boats returned drenched.

Parasols or umbrellas? An unusually quiet day outside the Pier Pavilion. (Pic. Sefton Libraries).

But, matching the mood of the triumphant speeches and the excitement of the crowds, the grey skies cleared, the sun appeared and by mid-afternoon the sea calmed a little and Storm King set off with her passengers to Liverpool.

Meanwhile the VIPs and guests, including mayors from the surroundings towns, returned to the town hall for one of the most sumptuous banquets in the town's history - soups, salmon steaks, fillet of sole, beef, turkey, chicken, lamb, duck, veal, tongue, pineapples, raspberries, lemon ices, strawberries, grapes, champagne, wines, Burgundy, port, sherry. It is recorded that wine in abundance was provided, fortification for the hours of more speeches and toasts, to the Queen, the success of the Pier Company and many others. Even Nelson's exhortation at the time of the Battle of Trafalgar for men to do their duty was quoted.

The speeches included a special tribute to Samuel Boothroyd who was credited with having conceived the idea of the pier and with his "indomitable energy and perseverance" had brought it to reality although Boothroyd graciously denied that he had produced the original idea.

The most obvious missing guest was Brunlees whose great masterpiece lay in darkness on the sands. By the day of celebrations he was working in South America.

By mid-evening the steamer passengers to Liverpool were on their way back, by steam train (return fare,

one shilling) to a town where the guests who had paid ten shilling and sixpence for the tickets, which included refreshments, were enjoying the music and dancing of the full-dress ball at the town hall. Outside the streets were lit with gas provided free for the new illuminations and by fireworks.

The ball continued into the early hours. When it ended among the distinguished guests a Mr. H. Bromilow gratefully went home. The strain of organising the huge procession, his "assiduous labours" had left him with a severe headache. As the jollity diminished others realised they would soon face the reality about the financial future of the pier.

Dr. Barron may indeed have talked loftily about how the pier promoters had not been concerned with "sordid pecuniary interests" but then it was not only the town's middle-class and others with money that had been at the front of the queue to buy shares in the Pier Company. The working-class too has also recognised the developing trend for visits to the seaside, helped by the railways and the money the pier would, hopefully, bring to the town.

So many ordinary folk, local fishermen, domestic servants, shop and office workers and others were among the supporters. Some had risked their life-savings in buying shares. It could bring a worthwhile return - or their cash could vanish like seashore sand in a winter wind.

When the pier opened for business they would begin to find out.

The Pier, Southport.

SPECTACULAR
SUCCESS

"You have the breeze and sea without the sickness and rattling or pitching of a vessel. It is there the girl gets the bloom in her cheeks again and the pale faces of the town a tinge of the sun."

B ut the pier was an immediate and spectacular success. Nothing like it had been built before. Earlier piers had been built essentially for practical reasons, for shipping. Southport's too was built for commercial reasons, for the steamers using the pier head. But essentially this was a new concept, a pleasure pier built for fun, for those who would enjoy a breezy walk across the waves. It was "the white knuckle ride of 1860," as a 20th century businessman put it.

A ticket for the summer season cost just a few shillings and for the promenaders, there were the summer stalls and the shows, the sounds of gaiety and laughter, the sea breezes, the wide, uninterrupted views for those who lives were spent in mean city streets, in the dreary surroundings of industrial towns.

Top-hatted gentlemen among the Sunday morning parade at Southport pier in 1865.
(Pic. Botanic Gardens Museum, Sefton Council).

As the writer of a Southport Guide Book at the turn of the 19th century put it: "A fine panoramic view may be had to Black Coombe in Cumberland, Lytham, the estuary of the Ribble, the Lancashire hills, the Promenade of Southport, the channel of the Mersey, the Cheshire Hills, the Ormes Head in North Wales and, to the front of the spectators, is the open sea. "The author suggested it gave the sensation of being on the deck of a ship at anchor in smooth waters.

A graphic image of the size, the popularity and sheer excitement of the pier in the second half of the 19th century comes from the Hon Mrs. Catherine Winter, an Irish barrister and authoress, who arrived in Southport in the winter of 1870. She was perhaps among those who had made the visit for the imagined or real benefits of the sea air and the waters because she was certainly very ill. If the sea air was actually beneficial they took some time to work.

The lady stayed indoors for three months, but as the winter turned to spring, by the following March she was able to make the journey along the tramway to the end of the pier. Her vivid impressions are recorded in Francis Bailey's *History of Southport*.

"Looking at the pier from the shore, I had no idea of its size; regular station-houses, covered seats, salons and shops are everywhere starting up to meet one's desires; so that if you can shop in Lord Street under shady bowers, you can shop on the pier in the middle of the ocean, while the promenaders are flocking in thousands on the walk reserved for them on the side of the tramway and Rowland and Sons' charming band are performing operas, pieces of music, quadrilles, waltzes and fast dances to no end. The end of the pier was large enough for several balls at once. How delightful it would be to dance 'On the wide, wild billow cast."

An impression of the town and the sands in the following decade was provided during a lengthy piece in the Illustrated London News marking the gathering of the British Association of Science in the town in 1883.

The writer hoped the "learned members and the leisured lovers of learning" would enjoy, with fine weather, the refreshing breezes of the Irish Sea and the attractions of "a newly built town on the sands at Southport."

"It is a very salubrious and rather agreeable piece of our western shores, a favourite summer resort, though not what is called bracing, of the Liverpool and Manchester commercial and manufacturing classes."

With the pier tramway and the spacious end platform visitors were assured that the sea was always accessible. It was also worth the train ride or the long walk because from the pier end "fine distant views of the mountains of Wales, of Cumberland and Westmoreland with sunset's effects of unsurpassed brilliance are obtained."

Also, then as now, children played in the sand hills. The sands were recommended as areas for magnificent walking or riding and for sailing boats on wheels when the winds were strong.

For those keen to take the waters, the sands were recommended for safe bathing with the aid of "machines."

Bathing machines had been introduced in about the 1730s, an idea similar to beach huts but with the refinement of being fitted with wheels. For the extra convenience and particularly privacy of the ladies preparing to change into bathing costumes, the machines could be hauled across the sands to the sea, a welcome distance away from the crowds. The machines remained in use until about the start of World War 1 in 1914 when they were succeeded by bathing tents, erected on the sands and bathing or beach huts on the promenades.

pic. Sefton Library

When the British Association came to town in 1883 Southport had a population of 35,000. The Illustrated London News correspondent described the town as "handsome, lively but never noisy." Whether it was seen as a compliment to the town or a mild complaint is uncertain but the correspondent added the thought: "If you want a bracing air we should say you had better go to Blackpool."

At the sea end, the pier had a platform 100 feet wide by 32 with stairs descending to the sands at low water which, it was pointed out, "provides a great acquisition for visitors wishing to encounter the breeze at the elevations of the pier or the milder air at the lower levels of the sands." Put another way, winds are stronger higher up.

While the pier was a huge benefit to steamer passengers, at times of extreme low water small boats had to be used to carry passengers to and from the steamers.

To meet the inconvenience the pier was lengthened by 260 yards, reaching the deep-water channel. The extension was built with platforms at different levels, making it possible to service the steamers, operating betweens the pier and Liverpool, Wales, the Isle of Man and elsewhere, at different states of the tide.

Nevertheless some still regarded the pier as inadequate and, taking advantage of the national seaside obsession with building piers, a project was launched to provide Southport with yet other pier.

Indeed plans were advanced for, not one, but two other piers. The scheme for the Alexandra suggested a pier several hundreds yards south of Brunlees's pier, also with shops, tramway and landing stage. More importantly, it would be 1500-1700 yards long, so servicing the steamers in deep water.

The other idea was for the Southport and Birkdale Crescent Pier which, starting at the southern end of the Promenade would be built seawards, not in the usual straight line, but, for reasons unknown, in a wide curve. The Alexandra Pier promoters presented their idea in a petition to Parliament. The design for the curved pier was shown in a local shop.

Potential supporters of either or both were cautioned by an observer who wrote to the local paper about the risks of investing in "our dangerous and tempest-beaten coast," Whether it was this or the protests of the existing Pier Company, naturally concerned about the financial repercussions of one and perhaps two rival piers, is not known but both pier projects became lost causes, little known pieces of Southport's history. The Pier Company was busy making improvements anyway.

If, for some, the pier had indeed been too short, for others it was too long. The length and the lack of shelter at the sea end caused complaints. Pier walkers were left abandoned to the weather and passengers arriving from the increasing number of steamers struggled with their luggage, waited for assistance, often in the wind and rain.

So in 1862 waiting and refreshment rooms were built at the pier head. The next year a track was provided down the centre of the deck and porters pushed the single carriage with the passengers' luggage to and from the pier head.

The positioning of the track in the middle brought complaints that the change ruined the pier as a promenade. So, encouraged by the huge popularity of the tramway, the Pier Company widened the pier and moved the tramway to the south side where it would remain until the early years of the 21st century.

The pier soon became well-loved by townsfolk and visitors. But it did have its critics. One wrote that it lacked any romantic feeling because the sea had receded so far that most of it was over land which was "a contradiction of what a pier is supposed to be." Indeed as the sea receded, by the late 20th century the pier passed over land, a boating lake, miniature golf course and then a road before reaching the sand and sea.

A crowd around Thoms Tea House at the Pier Head watch a pier diver in action.
(Pic. Botanic Gardens Museum, Sefton Council).

Then there was the lady Leila who wrote to the local paper the Southport Visiter in 1860 that the turnstiles were extremely inconvenient for elderly ladies especially when the amplitude of dress rendered it impossible for them to pass through the turnstiles without "much unpleasantness."

There is perhaps a hint of exasperation in the Pier Company's response, that the ladies should buy a ticket for a month or more, which would allow them to pass through the gate instead of the narrow turnstile.

These were indeed irritating niggles. For more importantly, as Bailey's history of Southport reported, "financially the pier was an immediate success." For some the magic of the pier was the theatre shows, the artists and the stalls or just the long breezy walk and a ride back on the rattling train, the line, as one pier customer put it, that Beeching could not close, recalling Dr. Beeching's restructuring of Britain's railways, meaning mostly line closures, in the 1960s.

Others were captivated by the wildlife, the feeding of the seabirds which, matching any end-of-the-pier conjuror's trick, appeared as if indeed by magic from the empty skies when the offal, collected from the fishermen and shrimpers, was tossed into the sea.

Henry Dawson in 'English Piers' wrote of the joyous freedom of the birds. "Nothing prettier can be seen anywhere than the scene that happens daily at noon at the pier head.

"For many years it has been the custom to feed the gulls at that hour so that nowadays every gull that is born within minutes of Southport comes into the world with a sort of instinct leading it to turn up then.

"Hundreds and hundreds of these lovely birds are daily participants in the feast and when their wants have been satisfied "Professor" Lloyd, the champion diver, gives a display of his prowess."

The early vision of the pier as a port for trade with industrial Lancashire faded but nevertheless the pier did develop a thriving commercial function.

In 1868 the tolls for mooring at the pier were listed as: For vessels, not a passenger vessel, under the burden of 100 tons, per ton 4d. Vessels of 150 tons upwards, per ton 6d. For other boats: Entirely open landing or taking on goods, per ton 6d. "Promenaders, those using the pier for walking, exercise or other purposes, except using the ships", were charged 6d. The use of bath or sedan cost one shilling, a pram sixpence. A journey on the train costs 3d, with an additional charge for luggage, for example, a penny for every trunk, portmanteau box or parcel and other packages up to 14 pounds.

Now in the dismal grey desolation of the lonely sea and sands on a winter's afternoon it is difficult to image that in the second half of the 19th century and into the 20th, the pier head was the gathering place for a huge armada of steamers, sailing boats, fishing boats, yachts, three-masted vessels and tugs.

In particularly the pier, now extended to the deep-water channel, had caused a huge expansion in steamer trade.

For more than sixty years ships would operate from Southport to Blackpool, Fleetwood, Preston, Barrow, Liverpool, Llandudno and Anglesey and beyond.

The biggest and best, the Greyhound, 230 feet long and 542 tons, sailed from the pier to the Menai Straits and to the Isle of Man. The Bickerstaffe too operated across the Irish Sea as Southport became the first mainland port to provide day return trips to the Isle of Man.

In 1866, four years after the pier opened, passengers could sail to Barrow for three shillings return second class, four shillings first class. In 1910 the return fare to Blackpool was two shillings and sixpence, to Llandudno three shillings and sixpence.

The first pier entrance in 1860. (Pic. Botanic Gardens Museum, Sefton Council).

The Southport Steamboat Company provided the twin-screw steamer Water Lily and offered sailings between Southport and Lytham daily, weather permitting and excluding Sundays. The single fare cost one shilling, the return one shilling and sixpence.

Sailing boats provided brief trips off the pier, perhaps for those with less time or, as the operators, chose to put it in an advertisement in the local paper, "to lovers of pure air without smoke."

The fishing boats would navigate the crowded waters around the steamers. By 1920 more than 100 were working off the pier, sailing to work the fertile fishing grounds around Morecambe Bay and elsewhere. The vessels included trawl boats, made in the Marshside and Crossens districts of Southport, designed to cope with the local shallow waters.

By the outbreak of World War 1, in 1914, the golden age of pier building was almost at an end. Most of the steamers were commandeered for wartime national service. When the war finished only a few returned. The end of the era of steamers appeared with the silting up of the Bog Hole and the South Channel and in the 1920s the last of the steamers sailed away, marking the final end to the dreams of eighty years for Southport to become a real port. The fishing fleet vanished too.

But for decades the pier had fulfilled the different ambitions of the early dreamers about a pier at Southport. It was a "fun" pier for those whose vision had always been for a pier as a promenade for a stroll or to listen to the bands, enjoy the sea breezes and the shows. Yet at the same time it met the hopes of those who thought Southport should have a commercial pier. It never actually, as some early planners hoped, a pier serving ships bringing goods to be carried by railway to Manchester but it did meet commercial interests in the steamer services and the fast-developing Southport fishing fleet.

The Pier Company continued with its ambitions. In 1903 the original entrance was demolished and the site redeveloped. Steam power was introduced for the railway, to transport luggage and then also for passengers, the first cable tramway for passenger traffic in the world. The line would later become electrified, before becoming diesel-powered after World War II and then, at the start of the 21st century, the train was replaced by a battery-powered tram. Plans for a second track remained, just plans.

The pier closed during World War II and searchlight installed, hopefully identifying German planes on bombing missions to Merseyside and industrial targets in northern England.

With the end of the war the pier reopened and the crowds returned. But the pier was never to recapture the crowds, the gaiety, the sheer class and style of Southport in the pre-war years. By day in summer the pier was a place for pleasure, of laughter and a great range of entertainments. At night it changed providing evening shows, a walk across the Marine Lake with the lights on the pillars in the lake reflecting in the waters, a graceful, splendid reminder of Venice.

But the pier was not free from disasters.

Within a few years of opening, in 1865, one of the tram cars left the line and Mrs. Frances Bateman, a widow, was hurled from her seat, thrown into the railings and died within 24 hours. Her brother-in-law John Anderton survived with serious injuries. Mrs. Bateman's representatives sued the Pier Company and received £400. Mr. Anderton was awarded £250.

In 1889 pier foundations had been swept away, the refreshment room wrecked in storm force winds and high seas. But storms were not the only threat.

In September 1950, the schooner Happy Harry became a prisoner of the winds of more than 70 miles per hour and, defenceless, was driven into the pier causing damage to the

Pier Pavilion.

pier structure and trackway. The schooner was beyond repair and was removed by explosions, pounds of gelignite, which scattered the ship's remains 100 yards around the beach.

But with wooden buildings and hundreds of yards of wooden decking, the real threat to piers was always fire and flames fanned by the winds. Southport's pier was as vulnerable as any other.

In 1897 a huge fire destroyed the pier head, the pavilion and other buildings in a blaze causing damage estimated at £4,000.

Another fire, in 1933, destroyed the seaward end of the pier, a blaze so severe the flames could be seen across the Ribble estuary at Blackpool, so dramatic people travelled from miles around in their cars to watch and residents on the Promenade came out still dressed in their pyjamas. The concert pavilion crashed into the sea.

The likely cause was a discarded cigarette. Damage was estimated at £5,000 - £6,000. While the Pier Company was insured, the ladies of the orchestra, booked for daily concerts, were not. Their instruments were destroyed. Copies of their music were last seen floating on the sea.

Yet a third fire in 1959 destroyed the pier head buildings, including the bar, restaurant and amusements arcade, in a blaze that cost an estimated £50,000. As a result of the big fires of 1933 and 1959 the pier was reduced in length to about 1,260 yards although it still remained the second longest pier in Britain after Southend.

In addition to three big pier infernos, fire also erupted backstage at the Pier Pavilion in the 1940s during a performance of J.B. Priestley's "Dangerous Corner" and the pier also suffered countless smaller fires caused by discarded cigarette ends.

But musical instruments and charred decking could be replaced. Wrecked buildings could be restored and rebuilt, like the replacement of the original pavilion, destroyed in the blaze of 1897 with a much more lavish creation.

But the greatest disaster for the pier was yet to come, in the post-war years. Pier inspections began to reveal bits of iron rusting in the salt air, fallen onto the sands and into the boating lake. The planking too showed the wear of a century of rain and winter weather.

The pier was simply rusting and rotting at an alarming rate. The great worry for those with an affection for the pier, and those concerned about Britain's heritage, was that there was not the money or the political agreement to do much about it.

Southport was forced to think the unthinkable. Its famous Grade 11 listed pier, the oldest and longest surviving pleasure pier in the country, the first iron pier, one of the top tourist attractions in the North West and as important to the holiday town as the Tower to Blackpool, might have to be demolished before it collapsed into the sea.

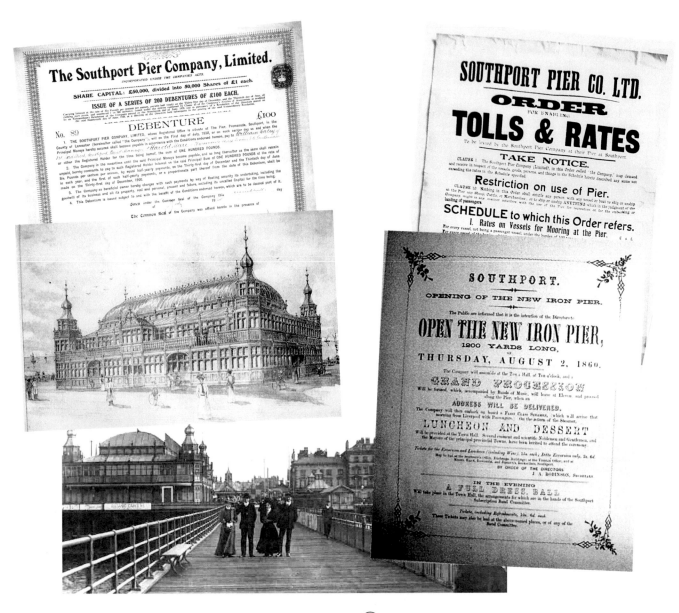

FUN TIMES

IN 1923 the last steamer the Bickerstaffe that had served Southport for almost 40 years, operating to Llandudno, Douglas and Barrow, sailed over the horizon and ended Southport's history as a port.

The end came with the silting up of the deep water South Channel which had been linked to the extensions of the Ribble channel revetment walls, the accumulation of dredging of the Mersey and the land reclamation between Southport and Hesketh Bank. For the same reasons the Southport Lifeboat Station closed two years later.

The jetties remained for the yachtsmen and, for a few more years, the fishing fleet. But basically with the departure of the steamers what remained was a real pleasure pier. It was what many of the originally town pier entrepreneurs of the 1860s had wanted anyway.

Thousands came on the booming railways and walked the pier, a temporary haven from the hardships of life in the towns of industrial Lancashire. In addition there were the more prosperous visitors, ladies and gentlemen dressed in the elegant styles of the wealthy folk of that era. The visitors to the prosperous, fashionable resort included also many of the famous, among them the showman and circus king Phineas Barnum, on holiday from America. Few would leave without the new pier experience.

At the dawn of the new century a local guide book and pier programmes reveal the pier in summer as providing one long round of amusements at the Pier Pavilion and outdoors at the pier head, the pier as a place of music and song. Big name stars booked into town and the Pier Pavilion. George Formby with his cheeky grin and honky-tonk ukulele brought smiles and laughter with "When I'm Cleaning Windows" and Gracie Fields a trace of tears to many eyes with "Sally." The Pier Company orchestra performed twice daily with sacred concerts on Sundays, timed to allow church attendance.

Mr. Seymour Richard's Imperial Pierrots provided concerts twice daily. Madam Blanche was part of the programme of summer entertainment leading a high-class ladies orchestra, the ladies all dressed in black. Through the years "Professor Osborne" thrilled thousands with his diving displays. Seawards there was the sight of the steamers which departed daily for Blackpool, Morecambe, Llandudno and elsewhere in addition to short excursions to sea.

The Pier Pavilion opened on New Year's Day 1902. The house was packed, as it would be on many more occasions, for the great stars of music hall and variety in the decades ahead - Marie Lloyd, the spirit of the music hall in the pre-1914 era, Harry Lauder, Jimmy James, George Robey, "the Prime Minister of Mirth", Wee Georgie Wood and Robb Wilton, George Formby, Gracie Fields and many more. Charlie Chaplin, dressed as a little lad in an Eton suit, appeared in a routine, which involved throwing crumbs at his fellow entertainers.

Some of the picture matinees were made of nearly two miles of film. The "beautiful picture entertainment" was extended to Sunday evenings although again with care that there was no interference with church attendance. The 1908 Grand National and Boat Race and the 1909 Cup Final were shown on film.

The original pavilion had been destroyed by fire in 1897. The new lavish and elegant building opened in 1902 and after alterations a few years later it carried the billing as "the most comfortable place of entertainment in Southport" and "one of the finest buildings in the north of England."

In the heat of the summer of 1911 it was also described as "the best ventilated hall in town, cool and comfortable." Reinforcing that claim, management provided free ice cream to those in the sixpenny and ninepenny seats during twice-weekly picture matinees.

Beyond the Pier Pavilion, the pier provided a world of sea breezes, the shriek of sea birds, pier shows, stalls, ice cream and shrimps, fortune tellers, kiss-me-quick hats, balloons, Punch and Judy shows and slot machines . . . .

But for sheer excitement Bert Powsey came top of any outdoor pier show.

The years between World Wars I and II were the times of the pier divers, such as Osborne who dived into the sea from the roof of Toms' tearooms at the end of the pier, "Peggy" Gadsby and Barney Pykett. Gadsby and Pykett, who was believed to have been a drummer boy in World War I, were both one-legged, the result of the years of trench warfare and slaughter in Europe.

But at Southport Bert Powsey - like Osborne, styled "professor" for unknown reasons - seems to have been the outstanding crowd thriller.

A card illustration of the manoeuvres of the famous pier divers including "Swan Dive" and "Somersault in Chair." (Insert) "Professor" Leslie Gadsby. (Pic. Sefton Libraries).

Powsey provided three shows a day, entertaining thousands with breath-taking performances, pedalling his bamboo bicycle off the roof of Rowntrees café into the sea, diving with his hands and feet tied or inside a burning sack, a Houdini of the waves, plunging into water set on fire with petrol and, most spectacularly, allowing himself to be set on fire and diving off the pier as the flames swept around his body. He was well experienced. One of his feats had included a 100 feet dive from a warehouse into the Thames.

Powsey, the son of a sailor, a petty officer on a sailing ship, was born in Sherness in 1866. He became an assistant in a grocer's shop and worked as an apprentice pipe fitter.

But he had gained fame at the age of 14 when he rescued a woman from drowning. At 24 he married the famous Rose Ellis who was then touring the country as the world's first deep-sea diver, making her appearances in a diving suit.

Crowds gather at the Pier Head to watch one of the popular performances from pier divers "Professor" Powsey.

Powsey went to Marlborough College and there became a swimming instructor before beginning his diving career at Herne Bay. He moved to Southport early in the 1900s and remained an attraction for more than 20 years, one of the pier divers whose performances one startled observer described as "maniacal antics."

Dressed in his black leotard, red trunks and red skull cap Powsey was a short, barrel-chested man with a Cockney accent who smoked a pipe and smelt of tobacco.

Sometimes he also smelt of petrol. Powsey's top act was to put cotton-wool padding on his back which was then soaked in petrol by his father or one of his sons before he dived from a plank into the waves. His other specialities included a dive from a 70 feet ladder into a tank eight feet wide, 14 long and only five feet deep.

Powsey travelled the country with his ladder and steel tank, sections bolted together and lined with canvas. The challenge was not just to avoid smashing into the steel frame but also to hit the water and come up and over the edge of the tank, arching his arms and back in one perfectly-timed, immediate movement. But he was an expert and held the world record for shallow dives.

In 1926 he visited Europe, America, Scandinavia and North Africa, part of a world tour taking his "dive of flames" to spellbound audiences in 18 countries, greatly admired by, among others, the distinguished historian, the late AJP Taylor who lived in Southport and described Powsey as his boyhood hero.

Prof. Osbourne diving from Southport Pier

One observer suggests that his dive in flames was not quite as daring or foolhardy as it seemed, that as Powsey plunged seawards the wind would sweep the flames away from his body and that anyway they were quickly extinguished in the water. But the risks in his long career were obviously real.

But he never had an accident. He was still diving into the sea in flames in his 60s, and he was 73 when he came out of retirement to dive into a tank for the last time for the Mayor of Southport's Forces Benevolent Fund early in World War II.

His last role was as a lifeguard at the Southport Open Air Baths. He died in 1956, aged 89, and left two daughters and five sons including two who, in a more limited way, carried on his diving tradition.

Powsey was long remembered by his fans and others. Certainly those he rescued from drowning at Herne Bay after the pier train ran into the sea remembered him, even if his reward from one woman was just one shilling. The two men he rescued from drowning in the infamous Bog Hole off the Southport coast had cause to remember him throughout their lives.

Powsey helped create one of the most enduring catchphrases of the mid-20th century.

When the pier divers surfaced their assistants weaved through the crowds, flat hats and bowlers upturned, in search of tips, with the cry: "Don't forget the diver." It was to become one of the most famous lines in the comedian Tommy Handley's popular radio show of the 1940s, ITMA. (It's That Man Again).

The grandeur and gaiety of the Pier Pavilion faded into memory too. The Pavilion closed before becoming an amusement arcade, a dodgem car circuit, a dance hall during World War II and a theatre before it was finally redeveloped as part of the new pier entrance.

But there was a lasting legacy from the shows at that end of the pier too. In 1929 the famous duo of Flanagan and Allan had written a sentimental little song and decided to test it for the first time on the Pavilion audience. "Underneath the Arches" was to become one of the greatest hit songs of the 20th century.

ROUGH TIMES

N OW in a time of less severe weather some of the storms of the last century are beyond imagination.

Records reveal winds of such fury sweeping the seafront that paving flags four feet long were hurled around like playing cards, how on one awesome day the Promenade actually vibrated side to side and sheets of water splashed over the roof of the old Victoria Hotel, opposite the pier entrance on the town side of the Promenade. Old photographs show the sea frozen, holding fishing boats as if in a vice screwed so tight some boats were splintered and crushed. Southport citizens of senior years can tell of wading across Lord Street, of the wooden blocks below the tarmac floating to the surface.

One of the outstanding pictures from the pier picture archives, "the Great Frost" of 1895. The sea froze so hard fishing boats were crushed.

Despite Brunlees's weather and waterproofing of the pier, within a century the structure was beginning to reveal alarming problems.

An employee in the Southport Borough Surveyor's department, accompanied by a surveyor, equipped with ladders and hammers, walked under the pier from the Promenade to the seaward end.

Many years later he recalled: "We were about ten days going down (an inspection along the length of pier) and the rust was falling like snowflakes. When arriving at the seaward end the surveyor gave his verdict: 'I'll condemn it.'"

But maybe Brunlees's great pier would have survived through the tempests, the decades of attack by the destructive mixture of sand, salt and sea air, if it had been adequately maintained and repaired.

The obvious dilemma for Southport, probably like many seaside resorts with an old Victorian pier, was finding the money for repairs at times of other urgent and expensive needs, such as education, housing and social services.

The result at Southport was simply that the cash was not there to maintain the pier, or it was there, it was never made available from town hall funds. Whatever the explanation, the pier received little more than sticking plaster treatment during the years when it needed major operations.

Several factors had come together to produce the crisis.

One was that in the post-World War II years the pattern of holidays in Britain changed. Many more holidaymakers went on cheap, short-haul flights to the Costa Brava or at least somewhere sunny. Far fewer were prepared to take a gamble on the weather in places such as Southport. So there were less people spending money in the town.

Also the then Southport Council operated a low-rates policy and with such enthusiasm that at one time it could claim domestic rates were among the three lowest county boroughs in the country. But this good news for the ratepayers sowed the seeds of a deep future financial crisis for the pier.

As the council struggled to keep rates down, bills went up. Inflation in the 1970s began to rise and by 1977 reached a crippling 27 per cent.

Funds for non-essential work, such as pier maintenance, began to dry-up. While the rusting structure needed urgent repairs, town hall costs were rocketing. As far as the pier was concerned there was the money to keep it safe but not much more. Even that fragile situation would not last.

Still Southport always has affection for its pier and indeed knows its economic value as a tourism asset. The pier cash crisis, though serious and escalating, might have been resolved if the resort had remained totally in charge of its own affairs.

But the early 1970s brought local government reorganisation, scrapping the single Southport authority and creating a new authority, Sefton, extending southwards from Southport to the fringe of the city of Liverpool.

The joining of the seaside resort of Southport with outer areas of the city was always going to be an uneasy marriage. It could never be otherwise. At one end Southport needed money for the attractions of a holiday resort including fashionable Lord Street with its fairy lights, Victorian arcades and pier, all worthy causes indeed for a holiday town. But at the city end of the new authority there were other very different but perhaps more urgent needs, such as schools and housing. When budgets were discussed a conflict of interests must have seemed inevitable.

The pier continued to be starved of essential funding and by the 1990s it was reaching the point of collapse.

Pier surveys could be carried out only in winter, when the

holiday crowds had returned home and the pier was deserted. Then men of the council engineer's section abseiled and scrambled around the structure, sometimes strapped in harnesses to inspect the girders, working in freezing winds, rain and frost. Their findings revealed the appalling extent of the years of neglect, missing and rusting ironwork on a huge scale, rotten planking. If the pier was to be saved it would involve a huge repair bill.

The decay reached the point where public safety became a matter of concern. In the 1990s it was closed for safety reasons, left abandoned to the sea and winds.

Yet it could not be ignored, allowed to collapse into the sea. Whatever options were considered for the pier, doing nothing was not one. The good luck which had so far prevented a chunk of rusted iron or a piece of rotten wood falling on the heads of holidaymakers strolling along the sands or relaxing in a rowing boat on the Marine Lake could not be expected to continue for ever. Then the council would face legal action and perhaps substantial damages.

Before that happened it seems certain that the Health and Safety people would have ordered the pier be made safe. If the council could not find the money for repairs then demolition would have to be considered which would cost hundreds of thousands of pounds and there would be nothing to show for that expense.

The survey work ended with the politicians given three choices. The pier could be restored at its full length. It could be reduced to half its length, retaining only the section across the sands and sea, which would reduce the repair bill and future maintenance costs. The other alternative was that it could be demolished.

In fact the choices were not that simple. If the pier was to be demolished, which many thought the best solution, that would cost about £500,000 and the holiday town would be left without one of its top tourist assets.

The council debate was a cliffhanger. Finally the council decided to keep the pier and at its full length. But it was a council decision taken without much enthusiasm. One of the finest piers in Britain, a great legacy from the Victorian age, was saved from the scrap yard by just one vote.

All that was needed now was to find the money for the huge repair bill.

THE WORK BEGINS

Workmen walked the decking, prodded the woodwork, scrambled around the web of ironwork, tapping the spars, in places using ultra-sonic testing equipment.

The depth of the crisis, the rot and the rust, was far deeper than had been anticipated.

Many of the cast iron columns, dipped in coal tar as a protection against the weather 150 years earlier, were in good condition, perhaps as many as 90 per cent. But for those determined to save the pier this was a rare piece of good news.

Elsewhere, columns, cut loose from the cross-supporting ironwork as the inspections and later the repair work began, were so rusted they simply collapsed onto the sands. Many of

the cracked columns would be repaired with a sleeve of steel fitted inside the outer iron case, spanning the crack, much like a splint on a broken limb.

But many of the lattice members, the cross-ironwork at the top of the columns, were also rusted or broken. Some were missing. Most of the corrosion was on the south side of the pier which faces the prevailing winds and, critically, supported the weight of the train.

While only about 40 of the 400 cast iron column needed to be repaired or replaced the early forecast that only 50 per cent of the latticework would need renewing was hugely optimistic.

Every piece would have to be replaced together with every plank of decking. In total, everything on the pier about the top of the upright columns would have to be renewed.

Brunlees's great seaside masterpiece, once regarded as "nearly indestructible," was at the point of total collapse. If the pier was to be saved from the demolition gangs it would have to be virtually rebuilt.

The great irony is that if crisis had developed perhaps 20 years earlier almost certainly the pier would have been demolished. The only alternative would have been the council somehow finding the money or some rich, pier-loving benefactor, arriving with the cash. At that time both were unlikely.

But if there was going to be a good time for the pier to have a crisis, here it arrived with perfect timing.

The first piece of good fortune was that the crisis came at a time when conservation was at the top of the national agenda. The save-the-pier lobby found the mood of the times perfect for its campaign.

But the most extraordinary piece of good luck was that while local government could not find the money and for years all efforts to get grants had failed, the pier was now collapsing at precisely the time there was the opportunity of cash to save it from elsewhere, including Heritage Lottery and also from Europe.

The tide of good luck continued to flow towards the pier.

The merger of Southport into the new local authority of Sefton had been far from popular among many in the resort who argued and campaigned for Southport to keep its historic links and remain part of Lancashire.

But Southport has become part of Sefton which was part of Merseyside which was an area for European Objective One funding. So the pier could be considered for European money. It would not have qualified if, as many wished, Southport had been left as part of Lancashire. As happened, the Merseyside connection was to prove vital in saving the pier.

But the drama was not finished. Heritage Lottery helped with the costs of survey work which revealed the size of the task ahead. Then came the devastating news - no more Lottery money would be available for Southport's pier.

The crisis now presented a financial disaster. Without Lottery money, European Objective One cash would not be given. Unless Heritage Lottery opened its purse the total save-the-pier cash plan would have collapsed. It seemed that all the anticipated grant money for the pier might just vanish altogether, like a toy balloon snatched by the winds from a toddler on the pier.

A deputation was sent from Southport to London and talks began with Heritage Lottery. Finally a solution was found.

Heritage Lottery had agreed to fund renovation work on Lord Street. But the Lord Street work could wait while the work on the pier could not.

The deal that saved the pier involved switching the Heritage Lottery money allocated for the non-urgent Lord Street project to the pier. That decision would also trigger the

release of other funds. Within a few years the Heritage Lottery money for the Lord Street work was also provided.

But the negotiations for money for the pier were long and detailed. It took four or five years to get the money together. But finally the cash came in from different sources, including Heritage Lottery and Objective One.

Sefton Council had been required to provide money too and finally gave £3.5million, a huge amount considering that in the preceding years it had given the appearance of hardly having the money to paint the pier. But then the council had no choice. If it had failed to provide its share the pier would not have received the money from Heritage Lottery and the European Fund, particularly valuable since these were grants, not loans, and the whole financial package would have collapsed leaving finally empty space on the sands where the greatest free attraction in the holiday town had been. If the pier had been just abandoned almost certainly Health and Safety would have insisted on its orderly demolition.

The work started with a contract for £4,106,000. But within months the contractor left the site and work came to a halt until a new contractor was engaged. Contract matters and simply the time the job was taking started to push up the price.

Pier building - and such was the dereliction that the pier was indeed almost totally rebuilt - is not an everyday experience for contractors.

But the new type of construction work did not present any difficulties other than at times a hostile environment, working with heavy steel in wind and rain among the girders above the sands and sea. But the pier was still a special reconstruction job.

The HL grant came with some conditions. One was that, in keeping with the heritage theme, the pier was to be restored, as far as was practicable, as it has been in 1860 and later years.

This imposed some restrictions on the workmen and sometimes the easiest, most convenient, perhaps cheapest way of doing a job, was not the most acceptable. But the work went ahead with real efforts to restore the pier faithfully to the past.

The upright columns, supporting straps and lattice work, were replaced as near as possible to the original specifications. Three different types of handrails were cast, matching those that had been fitted at different times during the last 150 years.

When men were working at the sea end of the pier they found chunks of metal and concrete buried in the sands, like the skeletal remains of some sea monster. The pieces, remains of earlier and long-collapsed work on the pier, were used to help make a new hammer-head structure at the pier head, complete with a bull-nose front seawards, in the style of the pier of the 19th century.

A pier tram, funded by the Mersey Waterfront Regional Park, the local council and the Pier Trust, replaced the pier train. A new pier train would have been more expensive and subjected to more health and safety considerations than a tram.

The tram is in the middle of the deck rather than in the position of the old train on the south side which, of course, had closed that side to pier walkers. The positioning of the tram in the centre of the decking now gives walkers the freedom to walk along both sides of the pier, with the changing views that provides, and has helped to position the lovely arch of lights extending seawards along the length of the pier which reflect in the waters in the evenings and brings again a touch of past elegance.

But the other reason the tram is in the middle is because

The modern pier tram. The environmental-friendly tram replaced a train and, like the first train in the 19th century, operates in the middle of the pier instead of the side.

this was the position of the first luggage train in 1860, another faithful restoration of the past.

The final cost was £7.2million. European Objective One provided £2.3m, Heritage Lottery £1.7m. and Sefton Council £3.5million. Southport Pier Trust also provided £20,000.

The Trust, made up of members of the business community, Sefton Council and residents, was set up as a means of accessing Heritage Lottery money. It also met Heritage Lottery wishes to see some evidence the public actually wanted the pier restored.

Ken Dodd attended a fund-raising lunch. A local girl made a sponsored parachute jump to raise funds. A well-known but anonymous resident gave a five-figure donation.

The modern pier pavilion.

But the biggest Trust money-raising effort, the big expression of public support, was the imaginative pier planks scheme, the invitation to the public to donate not less than £50 to buy a plank which would carry a suitable inscription.

The late Queen Mother bought a plank. So too did Ken Dodd and naturalist David Bellamy. A century and a half after Brunlees built the pier his descendants, in the United Kingdom and in Canada, bought planks and were reunited by the Pier Trust.

Schoolchildren bought planks as a reminder of their friendships with a displaced family from Bosnia who had stayed in the resort. A mother bought a plank in memory of her son who had died in a fire. Planks were bought on behalf of businesses and organisations. Many were donated in memory of lost partners, to mark birthdays, meetings or just memories. It seems some regarded the practical purchase of a plank as a worthwhile alternative to buying a seat or planting a tree in memory of a loved one.

Some raise a smile. One reads "Planks for the memory," another "Because no town should be pier less" and another "Southport has no peer."

Some are cryptic, the meaning known only to those close to the donor, such as "Have a good year and read Dickens" and "Keep on rockin, EFC" (Everton FC).

But the repeated theme is of happy memories including the romantic, such as "Walking with you, dear Skip." "Pat and Barry Rimmer, 40 years of love," and "What will survive of us is love, Rhona."

Some planks tell of passed meeting such as that of "Ron and Val Harvey" in 1966. Another makes a future appointment for Ric and Ki who will meet again on 24th of March 2025.

Perhaps a promise from a fortune teller to a romantic young lady telling of a meeting with a tall, dark stranger indeed came true and that the moment has been recorded in a plank somewhere among the many on the pier.

THE PIER REOPENS

THE pier was closed for four years before it reopened. It had been the biggest reconstruction job ever carried on a pier in Britain.

The restored pier - 1154 yards long - was made not of cast and wrought iron but steel and with a protective coating to last 15 years. The decking was of tough hardwood. The pier would not be allowed to rot and rust again although the maintenance job would be costly.

The repairs have been carried out with Green thoughts in mind. Some of the old, yet still solid, decking was recycled, sold to pier lovers as souvenirs or made into garden furniture. The new decking is from renewable sources. The new tram uses the latest environmentally-friendly, battery technology.

The pier divers and fortune-tellers have gone but new performers are expected to use the pier. Here a jazz band plays at the Pier Head.

The Heritage Grant had come with the condition that the pier must be free of admission charges and, with that, went any hope of the council earning some cash from a turnstile at the entrance.

But the council would at least have the income from the pier tram and from those given licences to operate the end-of-the-pier attractions, together more than sufficient to meet the pier operating costs, £70,000 a year on re-opening.

Indeed that amount of income provided a surplus, allocated for routine maintenance. In addition, crucially for those who had seen the results of the pier deprived of proper funding, decay to the point of collapse, the council would now set aside £50,000 a year for a major refurbishment every ten years.

A 'What the butler saw' machine is back too, in the pier pavilion, where, along with the café and a display about the surrounding coast of sands, sea and dunes, there is a remarkable old vintage penny arcade.

Here the pier visitor can change modern money into old pennies and play the machines which caused delight and amusement to visitors to the seaside long ago, machines which bring to life a laughing sailor and a haunted churchyard, tests strength and read palms and reveals what the butler saw or in this case what the butler didn't see. They are part of a collection of about 60 machines and the biggest collection open to the public in Britain.

The re-opening attracted great interest and enthusiasm with the number of visits counted in the tens of thousands. Visitors came from many miles to see Southport's grand new pier. Obviously after that great surge of interest the numbers were bound to reduce. But even in each of the following two years the number of pier visits was still considerably more than 300,000. That is the count only of those who those who walk or ride on the tram to the end. Since many, including mums and dads with tiring toddlers on a hot summer's

afternoon, walk only part of the way, leaving at the Ocean Plaza attractions and the start of the sands, the total number of visits is obviously much greater.

With the restoration came the accolades. The pier was voted Pier of the Year by the National Piers Society in 2003. It is not only Southport's biggest free attraction, but also one of the biggest seaside attractions of the North West. It is again that "light, airy walk" the Manchester Examiner found so enchanting in the original pier in 1860.

It is once again well-loved and for much the same reasons of the townsfolk and visitors a century ago.

There is the awesome vastness here, a breezy walk surrounded by sea and sands which in a busy, crowded world brings almost a sense of escape. The noises are again the sounds of wild nature, the laughter of children clutching ice creams or playing the slot machines, perhaps much like grand-parents and great-grandparents long ago.

Walking the pier on a hot afternoon or in the evenings when the lights sparkle in the water like scattered jewels other thoughts come to mind. One is that since the pier, like any other pleasure pier, does not go anywhere special there is no need to rush and so the pace of life is, thankfully, slowed, at least for a while. The other is that what has been made is not just a structure of steel and wood but, remarkably, a glimpse of the atmosphere of a distant age, a reminder of steamers and fishing boats, of great pier shows and more.

"And when you think what might have been," says a tourism chief. He was thinking of the meeting of the local council when the fate of the rusting and rotting pier was decided by just one vote. "If just one councillor who was in favour of saving the pier had not turned up for that meeting."

He meant that if that had happened then indeed it would have gone to the scrap yard.

As it was, a rare treasured legacy from the past, one of Britain's greatest piers, the first pier built for fun, was saved and restored, not just by the easiest, cheapest way either but with a fine commitment to recreating something rather special, a fine, elegant structure, a place of fun and laugher linked to the grace and style of past times.

It was achieved, with money, energy and more than a little good luck, yet also the sort of drive and dogged determination that made the pier possible by those other visionaries long ago.

Memories of Southport Pier

Southport Guide Book at the start of the 20th century

"You have the breeze and sea without the sickness and rattling or pitching of a vessel. It is there the girl gets the bloom in her cheeks again and the pale faces of the town a tinge of the sun."

Gwen, born 1914

*"I remember Powsey, the diver, riding off the pier on his bicycle. There was always a crowd to see him.
My grandfather played in the orchestra there in Victorian times. The pier had deck quoits, a telescope where you could look across to Blackpool and I remember the What the butler saw slot machine. I thought it was a bit naughty."*

Mabel, born 1924

"I went with mum and dad and it was a long walk to the pier end when I was a little girl. Sometimes I was frightened and crying.
I saw George Formby, Vera Lynn and others and there was a fortune-teller who had a crystal ball and everything.
My mother went to the fortune-teller every week for three weeks. It cost one shilling and sixpence, a lot of money then. Dad thought it a waste of money and waited outside.
But mum was worried about her son John who was in the Army during World War II, a prisoner of war. The fortune teller told her John would come home next week. But he never did and one day mum landed the fortune teller one, with her fist, for telling her John was coming home when he wasn't. But he did come home at the end of the war.
One day I went to the fortune teller too. I was told I would meet a nice young man, marry, live in London, have his children and be well-off. But I think the fortune-teller said that to every girl.
I did meet a few young men but I never did get married. I was too busy looking after the family."

Rita, born 1934

"There were always pier shows at the far end, pierriots, variety, singing, monologues, girls dancing. Then there was the ballroom dancing at the Promenade end.
The pier was a long walk for a little girl but over the years I do have such happy memories. My husband was a draughtsman and designed the old pier train, the Silver Belle."

Brian, born 1938

"A friend introduced me to fishing when I was in my 30s and I joined Southport Sea Angling Club and we used to fish off the pier. Not just men either, but women, husbands, wives, children. We had really great times. I was a member for 30 years. We went about once a fortnight for the fishing matches and they would last about three hours, an hour and a half each side of high water. There would be between 40 or 60 there for a match. We paid £2, £1 for the club and £1 for the "pot" and there would be a prize for the heaviest bag of fish and another for the biggest single catch. You could win maybe £20. There were some big matches. They would come from far away to fish off the pier, even from Scotland, four-man teams and there would be 30 teams.

You could get worms for bait from the sands, dig down for black lug and red lug. But whatever you used you did need to have the right bait, fresh. Also the best place to be was in the corner at the end of the pier so you could fish in the deep channels.

We fished for flounders, eels and bass in summer, codling and whiting in winter. My biggest catch was a one and a half pound eel but I know someone caught a seven-pound cod. If they were big enough you could take them home and eat them.

The night is the best time for fishing and while it could be cold we were well wrapped up. I remember the happy times. The other thing I remember is that a lad was fishing one day and saw a dead body in the water. Later we heard someone had fallen out of a boat off the Isle of Man.

I was chairman of the club for a while. My wife was a member too and one day we were walking out across the sands, two and a half miles to reach one channel and she sank in the sands and had to be pulled out. Her boots are still down there! The club started to fall apart when people came in who wanted to fish further afield. Husbands and wives did not want to do that or could not afford it and the club disbanded and then started again although people did want to fish in other places further down the coast around Liverpool.

Some go to fish off the rocks around the docks by Seaforth and some take a bottle of bleach to scatter around the rocks to keep the rats away. But standing on the rocks with the tide coming in, slip there and you've had it.

But Southport Pier was always easy and safe, a place for families to go fishing. If you took a break, went to the amusement arcade with the pin-ball machines or the café, sometimes you would come back and find a fish on the end of the line. It was such a friendly club, where everyone knew everyone else."

Pat, born 1933

"Times were hard when I was little and the pier was a special day out, once I got over the laughing figure at the pier entrance!

It was a clown or sailor or something like that, life-size and it frightened me. Also there were bumper cars. I went on them with my dad and I still remember the smell of the cars. In the amusement arcade I won a toy sailor. I had it for many years and loved it.

The pier had a coconut shy, a Gypsy Rose Lee, a telescope to look out to sea and a machine, which flicked pennies onto a board. You had to land the penny exactly in a square to win. It never did for me and even now I can remember the disappointment when I lost.

Also there was a What the butler saw machine, a woman on a chaise lounge. I think it cost two pence and as kids we thought it very daring. We used to queue up to have a look before the two pence ran out."

Albert, born 1927

"I went down the pier when I was about four and remember the fishing smacks anchored in the channel off the pier. At the pier end we used to sit in deck chairs and listen to the band and a singer called Babs. I remember she was a lady who was always laughing and she had a big St Bernard dog and she sang "All Over My Jealously." There was a tightrope walker too and, at the Promenade end, there was the Palace of Fun with lots of good variety shows.

Apart from fires, the pier was damaged when it was hit by a ship, the Happy Harry. The ship was damaged too and I remember the flames when it was decided that the ship should be set on fire.

Professor Powsey, the diver, was my grandfather. I saw him dive a lot including the time he came out of retirement for a dive at Princes Park, by the pier.

He dived 80 feet from a ladder into a little tank with five and a half feet of water, which must have looked like a postage stamp from the top of his ladder. But he had this iron-look in his face and when he hit the water he arched his body and arms straight away so that immediately he came to the surface. The surge of water swept over the sides of the tank. The intake of breath from the watching crowd was audible.

He had this stub of a cigar in his mouth and as he was about to dive he just took the lit stub inside his mouth, dived into the water and when he surfaced he sat on the edge of the tank, brought the lit cigar back out of his mouth and carried on smoking."

Rowland, born 1919

"My father was a postman and when he retired in 1926 he volunteered to be welfare officer for the Post Office veterans. One of the things he organised was for the veterans to meet on the pier.

They each bought an eight shillings contract for a year to walk on the pier and each day they used to meet at the second shelter to light their pipes, discuss Ramsey MacDonald (Prime Minister, formed Labour's first administration 1924) and the state of the world. They met every day, summer and winter, whatever the weather and it went on for years. You would think they had done enough walking in their lives!

There was the ladies orchestra at the end of the pier and a fortune-teller in the kiosk. She was dressed in a gypsy costume and charged sixpence. The servant girls crossed her palm with silver. Southport was full of servant girls then. There was an advertisement in the 'paper saying Southport was a growing seaside resort filled with cotton millionaires who required domestic servants. My aunt went to the fortune-teller. She told me that what she had been told proved exactly right, although she never told me what it was.

In the late 1940s Gypsy Petulengro came for a summer season with his orchestra and he too was a fortune-teller, famous because he provided readings in a national newspaper.

There were the sailing ships and the steamers and the shrimping carts. My dad took me fishing off the pier. In Nevill Street (the road leading to the pier) you could buy a line with 12 hooks for £1.

Sometimes when I never had two pence I used to climb onto the pier to get in free. Powsey was the most regular of the pier divers but there were others. They were called professors, like those who had the Punch and Judy shows.

In the 1920s Powsey was challenged by another diver to dive from a 'plane into the sea off the pier. Powsey thought it too risky and did not take part. The other diver jumped and broke his leg because there was not sufficient water.

Powsey had a vest with Bovril across the front. He was the only diver to ride his bicycle off the pier into the sea. The bike was tied to a length of rope so they could haul the thing back."

Mabel, born 1914

"I had a friend who used to give her elderly uncle a season ticket for trips to Llandudno by steamer from Southport pier.

He was Uncle Jack, an easy-going man, who had a business in Liverpool as a piano tuner. She used to buy him season tickets for his birthday each year. He really loved the sailings from Southport to Llandudno and back and then he would stay in the town."

Bill, born 1926

"I worked as a wheelwright for Southport Corporation for many years before I went into a career in education. We used to make carts, refuse barrows, wagons . . . I remember the day I started in 1940 because it was the day the first bomb fell on Southport in World War II.

I remember being on the shore with my aunt and seeing the big pier fire in 1933. But there were a many more fires over the years which were never reported in the 'papers because they were not big fires.

What happened was that when the pier decking planks were put down small pieces of wood were put between the lengths of planking, an easy way of keeping the same size gap between one plank and another.

But these spacers used to dry out in the summer and fall out below. People walking down the pier would throw down cigarette ends and these would fall into the gaps where the spacers had been and start fires. Much of the decking was pitch pine which went on fire beautifully many times. While they were not big fires, when it happened someone would just throw a bucket of water down and put the fire out.

I used to help the joiners replacing sections of the pier which had rotted or been destroyed in fire. During World War 11 there was a general shortage of timber and we went to Victoria Park where there were stands for the tennis courts where people could sit and watch the tennis, not really needed. These were made of Columbian pine and we pulled the stands down and used that to repair decking.

Apart from the joiners fixing the decking there was a steel fixer and a labourer who also had to repair the rusting steel work, not much more than a holding operation really, like the joiners with the decking, just keeping things going.

There was also a gang of painters, who used to work from one end of the pier to the other, chipping off the old paint and repainting with bitumen. They worked with chipping hammers and one of my jobs was to fix new wooden shafts. The gang used to work around the gantries, from one end of the pier to the other, out of season, in the howling winds and rains in winter. They did that every winter. There were about half a dozen men in the gang and I remember them all. I would not be surprised if some lives were not shortened with such a job in such weather conditions.

I also worked with blacksmiths. There was a channel running south west from the end of the pier. It was dangerous with the tides and it was known for the quicksands there too. So we used some steel barrels and put a plank on with the word "Danger" and went out in a rowing boat and put the barrels down with an anchor fastened to warn people. Kids had died out there.

When you see how big areas of the sands are grassing over, well, they will never be short of building land in Southport! Of course, we do not know what will happen with global warming, the effect on sea levels. Personally, I do not see sea levels rising but then who knows the way things are going, the way the grass is spreading. We could have a pier totally over land. Perhaps in another 100 years."

Allan, born 1937

"I used to go fishing off the pier with others from Southport and remember a competition about 20 years ago, an open event I think.

They were closing the pier. It was a Sunday, the end of the season. Anyway they had some beer left at the bar. It was 10p a pint and we drank the lot and went home legless. I don't remember whether I caught anything but you never caught a lot at Southport. The only reason we went there was to try and win a few bob in a competition.

But I remember one time when someone caught this big eel. It would have won the competition but it fell through the net and back into the sea."

Duncan, born 1962

"I used to come here as a kid and I remember that at the end of the pier there was a wartime mine, painted red and white, to collect money for charity. I did not find the pier a long walk even as a boy. But then I had climbed Ben Nevis when I was six or seven.

I worked on the pier years ago, then worked on shore patrols on the beach and now I am working here, a pier operator, driving the train and other duties. I met my first wife on the pier.

This (the big window of the pier pavilion) is my office window. Here the view changes every day. There is always something new. Some days you can see the snow on Snowdon in North Wales, the snows on the Lake District mountains.

Some people come here very regularly. One lady used to come most days and walk to the end on a zimmer frame on wheels. Then she would walk back again. I supposed she would have been in her late 80s. Then years ago, there was this regular, Hong Kong Harry — small chap in a tweed coat who seemed to have been in the army - who used to come and have a drink at the end of the pier. He came most days too. When the amusement slot machines were being moved in I did 22 trips over a couple of days helping bring them to the pier pavilion in a handcart.

In high winds you can feel the pier pavilion move. It is designed that way. The pavilion is a modern-designed building so it could not be joined to the pier which is a listed building. So the pavilion is actually separate, with its own supports.

The pier is a lovely place to work. There is the fresh air, lovely views. The scene changes ever day according to the weather. Some people look out of their office window onto a car park."

The saga of human endeavour, heroism and sacrifice surrounding the tragedy of the Mexico disaster recaptured in a Victorian illustration. The drawing was possibly a commemorative card, part of the fund-raising efforts in aid of survivors and dependants of those who died. (Illustration. Sefton Libraries).

The Mexico Lifeboat Disaster

For decades the pier has been a place for enjoyment, of smiles and laughter. But on one wild, awesome night in 1886 it became a platform where spectators watched a scene of tragedy and horror unfold in the surrounding waters.

The episode is a part of maritime history, Britain's greatest lifeboat disaster. When dawn finally lit the sands and sea, when the wreckage could be seen, bodies had floated ashore and others recovered from the waters, the cost of trying to save the stricken barque, the Mexico, became known. Almost 30 lifeboatmen had lost their lives.

On a night of rain, snow and hail, driven in great sheets by hurricane winds, the infamous sands of the Horse Bank, off the pier in the Ribble estuary, had claimed another victim.

The Mexico, carrying a mixed cargo had left Liverpool on the morning of December 5th in fair weather, heading for Ecuador and released her pilot at Anglesey. Then the weather changed.

Wind and sea forced the ship back. The anchor would not hold. Rigging and sail were lost and four days later she was fastened tight on the Horse Bank where terrified sailors had lashed themselves to the rigging and one remaining mast. There they awaited rescue or death in the mountainous seas.

Sometimes for those watching, from the pier or in the groups gathered below on the sands, the darkness and the storm blanketed the scene. But then the moon cast an eerie, pale light, the storm subsided, gathering its strength to be unleashed in renewed fury and it was possible to see the developing catastrophe.

In days of helicopters and powerful boats it is not easy to understand the sheer physical efforts involved in the next few hours.

With four horses, the Southport lifeboat the Eliza Fernley was dragged three and a half miles along the beach through the rain and sleet to a point where it could be launched windward of the Mexico through the surf.

Across the estuary, the Mexico light was also seen at St Annes where a watch was kept for distress signals and a lifeboat gun called the crew of the Laura Janet.

No similar watch was being kept at Lytham because it was thought no boat would be at sea in such weather. But two men out for a walk after dinner also saw the signal from the Mexico and the men of the lifeboat the Charles Biggs were also called, by knocking on their doors.

The Charles Biggs, a new lifeboat on her first rescue mission, reached the Mexico, hauled her sailors to safety and returned to Lytham to a tumultuous welcome. But she was the only lifeboat to return and in saving 12 sailors 27 lifeboatmen died.

Not surprisingly, the inquest verdict was accidental death. But with only two survivors from the Southport boat, not one from the St. Annes boat, the full story of what happened will never be known

But one theory about Southport's Eliza Fernley is that the launch was made with the oars tied in the rowlocks so that the men could start rowing immediately the lifeboat cleared the initial swell.

But when the boat was swamped in huge waves the men were entangled in oars. The boat capsized. The men were trapped underneath. Some drowned. Some suffocated.

Decades later Henry Robinson, one of two survivors from the Southport boat, remembered the wave, "the great greenback" that ended the lives of so many of his fellow Southport fishermen.

Another survivor, John "the Shark" Jackson, staggered off the beach and reached home almost on hands and knees where he collapsed in front of his wife, his body bloated with sea water.

Reliving the horror Jackson reported "Why mate, believe me but the weight of water alone was enough to have killed us." Robinson and Jackson each received £5 for their work that night.

But if the tied oars were one factor in the tragedy there was almost certainly another. Undoubtedly many men were not sufficiently young, strong or healthy to crew lifeboats through winter seas on one of the most treacherous shorelines in Britain.

Robinson was 52, Jackson 61. Among the men from St. Annes one was so riddled with consumption he was not expected to live to spring. Another lifeboatman had eaten no more than a bowl of gruel that day.

Many poems would be written about the events of that night, mostly reflecting on the bravery of the lifeboatmen "noble Christian heroes loving to do their duty" as one poet would write.

But sheer desperate need was also a reason brave men went to risk their lives to save the Mexico.

Lifeboatmen were usually fishermen, many with big families and often on the poverty line. In 1886 when a sailor received less than £3 a month lifeboatmen, such as those of the Eliza Fernley at Southport, could earn one-third of that for just one rescue. Usually payments were based on the time involved in a rescue.

The payment to the 16 crew of the Southport boat or since most were drowned, to their dependents, was 20 shillings, £1 each. For unknown reasons, the two survivors, Robinson and Jackson, received more, £5 each, for their work that dreadful night.

Payment for horses, usually hired from farmers to haul the lifeboats, was a set charge. Six horses had been hired at ten shilling each.

At Southport many of the dead, including those washed ashore like driftwood, by moonlight and on the morning tide, were laid out on straw at a seafront hotel. Sixteen widows and 52 orphans were made that night. The nation was appalled.

The disaster fund soon reached £50,000 with Queen Victoria and the German Emperor among the contributors. Many went to see the bodies and according to one report "it was noticed that the poor gave most freely."

The sense of tragedy is heightened by the fact that the sacrifice of the men of Southport's Eliza Fernley might have been unnecessary. It is possible the Lytham boat had already reached the Mexico and rescued the crew. But then in 1886 lifeboatmen did not have two-way radios, mobile phones, navigation aids, boats with powerful engines and lights able to probe the darkness.

The Mexico was salvaged, sold for £45 and towed to Preston docks for repairs. She went to sea again and was wrecked in another storm, off East Lothian in 1900. Again, the crew survived.

Items from the Mexico's cargo, including machetes, were salvaged and sold to souvenir hunters for the equivalent of 10p. The captain's sword and two sets of brass candlesticks became museum pieces. Chunks of cement from the ship were used as part of a breakwater on the Lancashire coast. Sheets of salvaged tin were used to keep dry the contents of a barn.

Yet there was a worthwhile legacy of that night and the loss of so many brave, poor men was not without value.

The disaster highlighted the poverty of Lancashire fishermen, the need for better lifeboats and led to the first fund-raising flag day in Britain for lifeboats, indeed for any cause.

The other legacy is society's enormous respect and admiration for men such as Henry Robinson and John "the shark" Jackson and of course, for their many brave successors who continue to risk their lives to save those in peril on the sea.

The Natural History of the Pier

THE surrounding sea, shore and dunes make up one of the most important coastlines in Britain for wildlife, an area, which includes five nature reserves, and other protected areas.

Southwards from the pier, the winds, waves and constantly shifting sands have established the biggest sand dune system in Britain, more than 2000 hectares rich in plant life where in summer the damp slacks are carpeted in flowers. Among them is the nationally rare Dune Helleborine.

This is also the home of large number of butterflies and moths and

Photo:English Nature

the dunes most famous resident, the Natterjack Toad, its call at the breeding pools in spring and summer echoing around the sand hills at dusk. About 40 per cent of the Natterjack population of the United Kingdom live in the dunes.

In the opposite direction, less than a mile from the pier, there is the most northerly home in Europe for the sand lizard and, beyond, the Ribble estuary is the second most important in Britain for birds, an area of international importance for waders. The Bar-Tailed Godwit, Knot and Sanderling are part of the great armada of winter visitors, birds on the passage south.

The coast is one of the most important staging posts in the United Kingdom for migrating birds, particularly waders and geese. The Common Ringed Plover and Lapwing are among the visitors but are also part of the permanent bird population, breeding around the pier.

The birds captivate walkers on the pier now as they did when the pier opened in 1860. Great gathering of Knot, like clouds blown on the wind, the sight and sound of the Pink-footed geese, from the far north, flying in formation like a great bomber force, are part of nature's great and free spectacular.

The scene looks unchanging. Indeed westwards and to far horizons, towards the Lake District and Wales, the views remain timeless. But around the pier the coast is undergoing dramatic change.

What is happening is part of the timeless story of Southport's shifting sands. The land is going through a process of accretion, moving out seawards, as it has for centuries. Lord Street was once in the sandhills and was developed in a dune slack, a flat area abundant with flowers in summer and flooded in winter. The shape of the old dunes can still be seen today, the land rising west and east of the slack, now the fashionable boulevard with its famous arcades.

Accretion to the north of the pier has allowed salt marsh grasses and plants to root in the new mud. To the south of the pier this process has been followed by sand dune grasses. So new sandhills were formed producing a scene much like that of Lord Street about 300 years ago.

But, curiously, while the winds and tides have brought deposits of sand, causing the beach around the pier to rise, the land to advance, just a few miles further south where the headland of Formby Point juts into the sea the opposite is happening. The land is eroding, mostly during storms. The sandhills are being demolished and action will have to be taken to manage this dune frontage as it moves slowly inland taking in cars parks and revealing old structure from times past.

One result of erosion has been to reveal footprints from thousands of years past, baked in the newly-exposed mud, wild boar, deer, and wild cattle. Prints of adults and children have also been discovered.

But what has been happening to cause the land to advance around the pier while coastal erosion takes place within a few miles?

Questions have been raised about the effect of years of sand removal from the Horse Bank in the Ribble Estuary, off the pier. But experts have different opinions.

Dave McAleavy, head of Coast and Countryside at Sefton Council, says: "The Southport coast is one of the country's most special natural areas and has been affected by natural change for many centuries. The very reason why Southport changed from a small fishing hamlet at South Hawes to a major resort town is wholly based on its natural value – the seaside.

"It is possible that if the coast at Southport continues to advance one day we may have a pier that is touched by the sea even less than it is it now. But then perhaps global warming and rising seas may bring the opposite result. Only time will tell.

"One thing is certain. We can do nothing to change the situation. Now, as always, nature will take its course."

The Future of the Pier

"Southport's Pier and its unique tram are part and parcel of what a classic traditional English seaside resort is all about. It is one of the key elements in Southport's redevelopment and move towards becoming 'England's Classic Resort.'

Of course, we need modern, quality-driven hotels, multi-screen cinemas, high-tech attractions and a wide range of restaurants and cuisine to cater for increasingly adventurous palates. But at the core of the resort are traditional attractions and features which include the pier and the architectural and shopping delight that is Lord Street.

The pier is a valuable part of England's national heritage and I have been delighted to see the way it has been restored. I look forward to local organisations using the pavilion at the end of the pier for exhibitions and events. Now that we have a transport system running from the pier head to the pavilion, people can make use of the facilities in the summer or the winter. This is one of the town's finest assets and I would encourage people to make use of it."

Tony Corfield, Head of Tourism, Sefton Council.   Autumn 2006

Acknowledgements

Among those who have given me much help and time in the making of "What the butler saw and all that" my special thanks go to Matthew Tinker, Local History Librarian and the staff of Southport Library's Local History Unit for their help in researching past events and providing pictures and also to Dave Richardson of Sefton Technical Services for guiding me through the details of the structural collapse of the pier and its rebirth.

My thanks also to Lord Fearn of Southport, John Cotterall, Tom Glover, Ralph Gregson, Phil King, Lindsey McCormick of Botanic Gardens Museum. Ramon and Albert Powsey, Phil Key, Graham Goulden, Richard Riding and others of the National Piers Society, Mike Swift of the Southport Pier Trust, Dave McAleavy of Sefton Council Coast and Countryside and also to those who have kindly loaned pictures and postcards and to the senior citizens of Southport, in homes for the elderly and elsewhere, who have shared their memories of long-distant days on the pier.

Harold Brough   Autumn 2006

Harold Brough

Harold Brough was brought up in Southport and has fond boyhood memories of breezy summer days, penny slot machines, long walks to the end of the pier and the welcome train ride back again.

He was on the staff of Southport newspapers, leaving to work on daily 'papers in Durham, Newcastle-on-Tyne and London before returning to Merseyside to join the Daily Post, Liverpool where he was Chief Features Writer.

He lives in Southport and works as a freelance journalist.

He is married with three grown-up daughters and has a passionate addiction to fellwalking, cycling and golf.

What the Butler Saw and All That is his first book on local history.